BEGINNER'S GUIDE TO KIRIGAMI

24

SKILL-BUILDING PROJECTS
USING ORIGAMI & PAPERCRAFTING SKILLS

Ghylenn Descamps

Fox Chapel
PUBLISHING

CONTENTS...

... VISUALS

CHAPTER 1: MAKING A START

1) FIRST CHRISTMAS TREE   2) PAIR OF VASES   3) PRETTY DRAGONFLY   4) CAKE TOPPER

5) PETAL GIFT BOX   6) LOVE POP-UP CARD   7) STYLISH LANTERN   8) TWO-COLORED BOXES

CHAPTER 2: DEVELOPING SKILLS

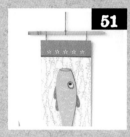

CHAPTER 3: LITTLE CHALLENGES

PREFACE

When my publisher suggested I do a book on kirigami, I literally jumped for joy! It's everything I love – beautiful papers, cutting and folding – sprinkled with a generous dose of Japanese inspiration. I couldn't wait to get started on some new creations . . .

But what exactly is kirigami?

Kirigami, from kiru, to cut, and gami, paper, is inspired by one of China's oldest traditions, "jian zhi," the art of paper cutting. Once reserved for the religious elite for use in rituals, it gradually spread to all levels of society. Jian zhi is still practiced during the Chinese Springtime Festival and New Year celebrations.

Jian zhi eventually made its way to the shores of Japan, where it was enriched by the paper-folding art of origami and evolved into what we now call kirigami.

A new dimension unfolded quite unexpectedly while I was working on my models. As I quietly cut and folded, I became very centered. I felt as though I were taking a quiet stroll down a path that soothed my spirit. It was an interior journey very much like meditation, an opportunity to breathe in a turbulent world.

It is this same Japanese-inspired creative journey that I invite you to experience as you make your way through this book and discover the marvelous art of kirigami.

Breathe, and be inspired by the papers of the Far East . . .

Ghylenn

ghylenndescamps.com

BASIC MATERIALS

Kirigami is a technique that requires only a few basic materials to start: paper, a cutter, and a cutting mat. There are more tools that will make it easier to perfect your skills. Investing in quality materials will help you acquire precision and speed, feel more relaxed, produce work of higher quality, and enjoy the experience so much more!

Here is a list of the materials used to make the projects in this book:

- Scalpel, aka craft knife (X-acto®-style tool with removable blades), and replacement blades
- Cutter, aka utility knife, and replacement blades
- Silhouette scissors (small scissors with thin blades and pointy tips)
- Scissors
- Metal ruler to guide cutter for straight cuts
- Cutting mat
- Paper-folding tool, aka bone folder, made from bone or plastic, for sharp creases
- Embossing stylus for scoring paper before folding
- Masking tape for securing the pattern to the paper to be cut without damaging it
- Glue gel that won't wrinkle paper
- Repositionable spray adhesive
- Permanent spray adhesive
- HB pencil or mechanical pencil
- Clean pencil eraser
- Printer
- Photocopier

Although the following tools are not essential, they will make the work easier:

- White pencil for tracing on dark paper
- Compass
- Compass circle cutter
- Hole punch
- Eyelet punch for making small, uniform holes
- Tweezers for gently removing cutout pieces of paper

And for pleasure:

- Decorative-edge scissors for making original cutouts and edges
- Disc cutter with punches in assorted shapes
- Sewing or tapestry needles for making very small holes

ABOUT THE PAPER

Paper is the essential element in kirigami! There is a variety of beautiful decorative papers that are sure to inspire you. It's important to choose the right paper, however, because not all of them are easy to cut. The wrong paper can make the work difficult and your project a disaster!

A few tips for choosing paper

The best paper to start out with is plain, smooth paper with a weight of 120 to 160 g. This type of paper is ideal for kirigami because it holds up well, is easy to cut, and comes in a wide variety of colors. It can also be used in a printer, which simplifies reproducing a pattern.

For models that need sufficient strength to stand, as in the case of boxes, it's better to use paper that weighs at least 210 g. Any shapes to be cut out, however, will need to be simplified, because this thicker paper will be more difficult to cut.

Tracing paper

This paper is essential for tracing and reproducing a pattern if you don't have access to a printer or photocopier. Tracing paper can also be used as a translucent layer underneath a cutout pattern, for example, in a lantern. This paper comes in different colors.

Patterned paper

It's tempting to use patterned paper, because some of them, particularly the Japanese papers, are truly magnificent. Here again, the choice is important: prints that are too vivid with highly contrasting colors risk ruining the final result by detracting from the cutout areas. It's all a question of balance. You can temper the overall effect by using plain-colored paper as a complement, or by using tone-on-tone patterned paper.

Combining two colors

Certain paper combinations give a boost to their creations. If you choose two papers for bicolor effect, you can choose two highly contrasting colors, like red and black, or a softer combination, like white and light blue.

Other papers . . .

You can choose from fiber-based or handmade papers, such as the Nepalese and Indian papers, which come in shimmering colors. These papers are often thick and difficult to cut, so avoid fine cuts that will needlessly tire out your hand and quickly use up your blades. These papers are, however, very easy to use if they are to be glued underneath a cutout, adding a decorative and aesthetically pleasing element to your project.

In short, feel free to try out a wide variety of papers until you understand the differences and determine your preferences.

US AND EUROPEAN PAPER SIZES

In the United States, common sizes of paper include letter (8½" x 11" / 216 x 279 mm) and half letter (5½" x 8½" / 140 x 216 mm), which is half the height of letter; many square sizes are also common. In Europe, paper is sized in the A series, with A4 (8¼" x 11 ¹¹⁄₁₆" / 210 x 297 mm) being the standard size for most letterhead and copy/printer paper, the equivalent to US letter paper. A5 (5 ¹³⁄₁₆" x 8¼" / 148 x 210 mm), the equivalent to US half letter, is also common. Be consistent with the paper system you use, and don't mix US system paper sizes with European system paper sizes, as they are very close in size but not identical.

Before You Begin

The first tip before you begin is to find a comfortable position. Kirigami requires concentration, precision, and patience. A calm, well-lit, and uncluttered area, having your tools and supplies within easy reach, and knowing how much time you have are also important considerations if you want your session to be productive. Craft knives and cutters are very sharp tools. It's easy to cut yourself if you are inattentive, so handle them with caution and don't rush!

GETTING FAMILIAR WITH THE TOOLS

Kirigami starts with learning how to use the cutters, each of which has its use and advantage. You should know how to hold and use them correctly in order to achieve your desired result under the best possible conditions.

Correct posture for holding a craft knife

A craft knife is held like a pen. Keep your wrist loose and use light pressure to cut the paper. When you press too hard, you can damage the paper and tire out your hand much faster. The craft knife serves mostly for delicate, complex, and curved cuts.

Your free hand should hold the paper on the cutting board. Keep this hand out of the path of the knife at all times.

Correct posture for holding a utility knife

A utility knife is held like a knife, with the hand on top of the tool. It is very practical for cutting straight lines along a ruler and for cutting large, simple curves.

Knife Helpers
Utility and craft knives are used on a self-healing cutting board. This cutting board will greatly lengthen the lives of the blades, keep paper from slipping, make cutting easier, and protect your work surface.

A metal ruler will prove much more durable against knife cuts and is much more stable while making long cuts or cutting thick paper.

Knife Blades
When using knives, you will need to change the blades regularly—papercutting takes its toll, dulling a blade's cutting edge. When you feel like the blade is scraping or pulling the paper instead of cutting it cleanly, or when you feel you have to press harder than you should, it's time to change the blade. Sometimes you may find you need to change the blade every hour! The goal is simply to keep the act of cutting comfortable and easy.

There are also ultra-resistant zirconium blades that are quite expensive, but which dull much slower.

WORKSPACE AND COMFORT

Here are a few lines to print and then practice on with the cutter and scalpel.
This exercise will help you master the technique of paper cutting, understand the
differences between the two types of knives, and find the most comfortable position.

Directions

Make two photocopies of the exercises on the left or scan and print them twice on 160 g paper. This will allow you to practice with the cutter, and then with the scalpel. Use the cutting mat.

Hold the sheet in place with your other hand, ensuring that hand is not in the way of the knife.

Start with the cutter to cut the straight lines: place the metal ruler along the line to be cut. Hold the ruler down firmly. This will help keep both the paper and the ruler in place. Slide the cutter along the edge of the ruler to cut the paper.

Cut out the other shapes. Use the metal ruler and cutter on the straight segments and large curves. Use the scalpel on the small curves.

Try varying the amount of pressure you put on the blade when cutting the paper. This will help you determine your preferences.

More tips

When starting out, it's normal to tense up. You may feel as though you have to press down hard to cut the paper. Blades have been known to bend or even break under the pressure of your hand! It's better to go over the paper with the knife several times than to press too hard. Over time, you will learn how to conserve your energy and become more efficient.

Take a break regularly, every hour, to rest your wrist or whenever you feel tension building up. It's important to remember to keep your wrist supple and relaxed so you will be more comfortable as you are cutting.

A common mistake

When you start out, a common mistake is to interrupt the cut too soon, or else cut too far. For best results, it's better to interrupt the cut and then add another cut to finish it.

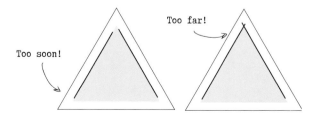

Too soon!

Too far!

PREPARING THE MODELS

There are a number of ways to prepare your patterns according to your preferences:

1) Print or photocopy the pattern on a sheet of plain copy paper.

In this case, cut out the pattern roughly, leaving a margin of ⅜" (1 cm) outside the pattern.

Apply repositionable spray adhesive to the back of the pattern. Glue it to the back of the paper you have selected.

The paper you choose should have a maximum weight of 80 to 120 g, because the pattern will increase the thickness of the element you will need to cut.

2) Print or photocopy the pattern directly on a sheet of colored paper using the photocopier or printer, then cut out the pattern.

3) If you don't have access to a printer or photocopier, use a sheet of tracing paper and a pencil. Trace and transfer the pattern onto the selected paper. Remember to use a light yellow or white pencil if you have chosen dark colored paper.

....

For letters

In kirigami, the patterns are inverted in order to hide the cut lines and the dotted lines that mark the folds in the final result. If you want to cut out letters, don't forget that the final result will be inverted. You will need to trace or print the letters as a mirror image in order to read them correctly once they have been cut out.

Letter model

Cutting

Final result

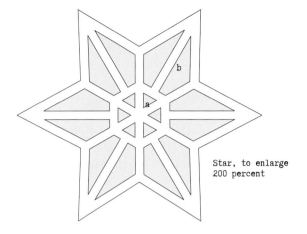

Star, to enlarge
200 percent

CUTTING STRAIGHT LINES
TIPS IN THE PHOTOS

✳ ✳ ✳

Star

Here is an exercise for cutting out a star that you can follow step-by-step in the photos. Since this model consists uniquely of segments, it will be easier to cut using the cutter and metal ruler.

Directions

Print the pattern on a sheet of 160 g colored paper (enlarged 200 percent). Lay the printed star on the cutting mat.

Start by cutting out a triangle from the inner (a) section: position the metal ruler along the line to be cut. Press down firmly on the ruler, which will hold the paper as well as the ruler in place. Slide the cutter along the edge of the ruler to cut the paper.

Cut out all the triangles from the inner (a) section of the star. If necessary, use the cutter to cut again if the triangles don't detach easily. Be careful not to cut past the line.

Cut out all the shapes from the outer (b) section of the star. Remove the pieces.

Place the star on a sheet of patterned paper. Hold it in place with masking tape. Cut out the contour of the star using the cutter and ruler. The two layers of paper will be cut out at the same time.

Glue the star onto the patterned paper using the glue pen.

CUTTING CURVES
TIPS IN THE PHOTOS

Flower

Here is an exercise for cutting out a flower that you can follow step by step in the photos. Since this model consists of curves, it will be easier if you use the scalpel. Hold the scalpel like a pen and don't let it get caught on the ruler. Cutting this model requires a fair amount of dexterity, but the repetitive nature of the cuts will be good practice for you.

Directions

Print the flower pattern on a sheet of 160 g colored paper. Lay the printed flower on the cutting mat. Enlarge it 200 percent if necessary.

Although it is usually better to cut out the center first, in this case you will save this step for last. This will help the paper hold together and make the cutting easier.

The trick is to use an eyelet punch to cut out the small circles at the end. This will produce the best results, and it's quick and easy.

1) Start by cutting the tip of the petal. Hold the sheet of paper with your other hand.

2) Cut by moving the scalpel toward you and toward the rounded end of the petal.

3) Turn the sheet of paper as you cut the round part.

4) Turn the sheet of paper again to finish cutting out the petal.

5) Remove the petal. If it is difficult to detach, use the cutter again to avoid tearing the paper.

Be careful not to cut past the traced lines. When the cutout pieces are very small, use tweezers to remove them. Continue cutting out the rest of the petals in the same fashion.

The flower, to be enlarged to different sizes to practice cutting.

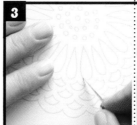

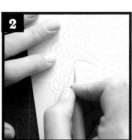
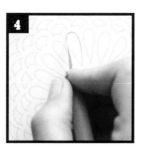

FOLDING

Folding is the complementary stage in kirigami.
This stage also requires precision to obtain the best results.

✳ ✳ ✳

It is recommended that you prepare the folds before cutting, as the paper holds up better before it is cut. There are two types of folds. Here are the symbols indicating the direction in which to fold the paper:

Valley fold

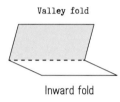

Inward fold

Mountain fold

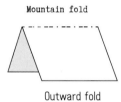

Outward fold

A cut line is represented this way : ———

TIPS IN PHOTOS

Here is an exercise to familiarize yourself with folds.

1) Print the pattern on a sheet of 160 g colored paper or trace the reference lines. Cut the two solid lines using the cutter and metal ruler on the cutting mat.

2) Mark the folds in dotted lines using the embossing stylus. Place the metal ruler along the dotted line and trace the line while pressing down.

3) Keep the ruler lined up with the fold to be made. Slide the paper-folding tool under the paper, pressing against the ruler to lift the paper and mark the fold. (Fold no. 1).

4) Turn the sheet of paper 90 degrees. Slide the paper-folding tool under the paper and mark Fold no. 2.

5) Once all the creases are pre-folded, fold the paper and flatten the creases with your hand. Press down each crease firmly using the paper-folding tool.

6) Open the sheet of paper to see the final result.

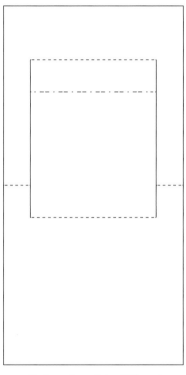

To be enlarged to different sizes for you to practice.

GLUING

Here are some tips on how to use glue.
Not all types of glue are multi-purpose.

For gluing small paper surfaces, use glue gel that won't wrinkle paper.

Double-sided adhesive rollers are very easy to use and there is no need to wait for the glue to dry.

Glue pens are practical for gluing extremely fine surfaces, and they don't drip.

Spray adhesives:
Use repositionable spray adhesive to attach the patterns to the back of the paper to be cut. Permanent spray adhesive can be used to reinforce very thin and fragile paper, for attaching a base to a card, and for gluing very fine cutouts together.

If you use spray adhesive regularly, it's a good idea to construct a glue box.

Use a clean cardboard box. Line the inside with newspaper.

Place the item to be glued inside the box, with the front lying on the newspaper. Shake the can of spray adhesive. Tilt the glue box and evenly spray the surface of the item to be glued.

It's better to use spray adhesive outdoors or in a well-ventilated area. Remove the item and immediately apply it to the desired position.

Smooth with your hand, pressing down to make it adhere.

A FEW TIPS

- Before starting a project, make sure you have enough time to complete it, and check that you have all the materials at hand.

- If you don't have exactly the paper that is recommended, select a paper that is equivalent to it.

- Feel free to simplify your project according to the time you have available.

- In short—have fun and let your imagination run wild!

MAKING A START

FIRST
CHRISTMAS TREE

FIRST CHRISTMAS TREE

SUPPLIES

1 sheet half letter/A5 verdigris paper
1 piece white glitter crafting tape
1 piece tracing paper

MATERIALS

Scalpel · Cutter · Scissors
Cutting mat · Masking tape

DIRECTIONS

1) Photocopy the two Christmas tree patterns on a sheet of copy paper. Cut out the Christmas trees roughly.

2) Lay the Christmas trees on the sheet of verdigris paper. Hold them in place using masking tape.

3) Place the verdigris paper on the cutting mat. Use the scalpel to cut out the stars and then gently remove them. Use scissors to cut out the Christmas trees. Cut the slots along the dotted lines. Detach the patterns.

4) Assemble by fitting the slots of the two trees together.

5) Trace the star pattern. Transfer it to a piece of white glitter crafting tape. Remove the protective film and glue the star to the top of the Christmas tree.

CHRISTMAS TREE
actual size

STAR
actual size

PAIR OF VASES

PRETTY DRAGONFLY

PAIR OF VASES

SUPPLIES FOR 2 VASES

1 sheet 160 g letter/A4 off-white Ingres paper
1 sheet letter/A4 green and white patterned Japanese (origami) paper

MATERIALS

Scalpel · Cutter · Metal ruler · Pencil
Cutting mat · Repositionable spray adhesive · Glue gel · Paper-folding tool · Embossing stylus

DIRECTIONS

1) Fold the sheet of off-white paper in half.

2) Photocopy the model of the vase on a sheet of copy paper. Cut along the dotted line using the cutter and ruler.

3) Apply repositionable spray adhesive to the back. Glue it to the sheet of off-white paper, ensuring the dotted line is lined up with the fold in the sheet. Smooth with your hand.

4) Cut the indicated lines using the cutter and metal ruler on the cutting mat.

5) Cut out the contour of the vase.

6) Position the edge of the ruler along a dotted line. Mark the line using the embossing stylus. Slide the paper-folding tool under the paper, pressing against the ruler to lift the paper and mark the fold. Remove the ruler. Flatten the crease using the paper-folding tool. Mark all the creases the same way. Remove the pattern. (See explanations on page 12.)

7) Open the vase slightly and invert the creases one by one, pushing them toward the interior of the vase. Press each crease firmly as you go along. Open the vase, then pinch the middle creases together to mark them. Fold the vase again, then flatten it entirely.

8) Cut out a 5 15/16 x 6 5/16 in. (15 x 16 cm) rectangle from the sheet of green and white patterned origami paper. Fold it in half and flatten the crease using the paper-folding tool.

9) Glue the back of vase, lining up the middle creases. Be careful to glue only one strip out of two. Cut off the excess paper, following the contour of the vase.

10) Trace the three small flowers. Transfer them to a piece of green and white patterned Japanese paper. Cut out the inner parts using the cutter on the cutting mat. Cut out the flowers. Glue them to the vase.

PRETTY DRAGONFLY

SUPPLIES

1 sheet 160 g 6⁵⁄₁₆ x 6⁵⁄₁₆ in. (16 x 16 cm) off-white paper
1 sheet 6 ¹¹⁄₁₆ x 6 ¹¹⁄₁₆ in. (17 x 17 cm) gold paper

MATERIALS

Scalpel · Cutter · Metal ruler · Pencil · Cutting mat
Repositionable spray adhesive · Glue gel or double-sided adhesive roller · Embossing stylus · Paper-folding tool

DIRECTIONS

1) Photocopy the dragonfly and flower patterns on a sheet of copy paper. Cut out the patterns.

2) Apply repositionable spray adhesive to the back of the patterns. Center and glue the patterns to the back of the sheet of off-white paper. Smooth with your hand.

3) Cut out the details of the wings and the small flower using the scalpel on the cutting mat. Gently remove the cutout pieces.

4) Cut out the contour of the wings, without cutting the dotted fold lines.

5) Mark the fold of the wings: position the edge of the ruler along a dotted line. Mark the fold using the embossing stylus. Slide the paper-folding tool under the paper, pressing against the ruler to lift the paper and mark the fold. Remove the ruler. Use the paper-folding tool to flatten the crease. Mark the other wing the same way. (See explanations on page 12.)

6) Cut out the body of the dragonfly and the antennae. Gently remove the cutout pieces.

7) Coat the back of the off-white card with adhesive, without applying glue under the wings. Center and apply it to the piece of gold paper. Open the wings toward the front of the card to make it three-dimensional.

DRAGONFLY
actual size

FLOWER
actual size

CAKE TOPPER

PETAL GIFT BOX

CAKE TOPPER

SUPPLIES

1 sheet 160 g half letter/A5 old rose paper
1 sheet 120 g half letter/A5 glazed chestnut paper
3 small wooden skewers

MATERIALS

Scalpel · Cutter · Metal ruler · Pencil
Cutting mat · Repositionable spray adhesive · Glue gel
Eyelet punch · Masking tape

DIRECTIONS

1) Photocopy all the letters on a sheet of copy paper. Cut out each letter roughly, leaving a margin of about ¼ in. (5 mm).

2) Apply repositionable spray adhesive to the back of the letters. The cutout letters are inverted. Position the full letters on the back of the sheet of old rose paper. Position the half-letters on the back of the sheet of glazed chestnut paper. Smooth with your hand.

3) Cut out the diamond shapes using the scalpel on the cutting mat.

4) Cut out the circles using the eyelet punch.

5) Cut out the contour of the letters using the scalpel on the cutting mat. Remove the patterns.

6) For each letter, glue the glazed chestnut piece onto the old rose letter as shown.

7) Flip over the letters. Attach a small wooden skewer to each letter and hold it in place with a piece of masking tape or a piece of paper coated with glue gel. Hold in place until the glue has dried.

LETTERS
actual size

2 TIMES

If you choose
a different word
for your topper, adapt
the same principle
for the other
letters.

PETAL GIFT BOX

SUPPLIES

1 sheet 11 ¹³⁄₁₆ x 11 ¹³⁄₁₆ in. (30 x 30 cm) yellow and white patterned Japanese paper
1 sheet 11 ¹³⁄₁₆ x 11 ¹³⁄₁₆ in. (30 x 30 cm) red paper

MATERIALS

Scalpel · Cutter · Metal ruler · Paper-folding tool
Pencil · Cutting mat · Repositionable spray adhesive
Permanent spray adhesive · Glue gel

DIRECTIONS

1) Photocopy the box pattern on a sheet of copy paper.

2) Apply repositionable spray adhesive to the back of the pattern. Glue it to the back of the sheet of red paper. Smooth with your hand. Cut out the box.

3) Mark the folding lines on the box. Position the edge of the ruler along each dotted line. Slide the bone folder along the line. Remove the ruler. Remove the folds with the bone folder. (See p. 12.)

4) Gently remove the pattern from the red paper.

5) Spray the side already coated in repositionable spray adhesive with permanent spray adhesive. Apply it to the back of the sheet of yellow and white Japanese paper. Smooth with your hand.

6) Mark all the folds again as previously explained, using the creases made on the red sheet to line them up perfectly. Cut off the excess paper.

7) Assemble the box. Apply glue gel to the flaps, then glue the flaps to the sides of the box to make it stand up. Hold in place until the glue has dried.

8) Close the box by folding the red petals as shown. Slip the last petal under the first to close the box.

BOX
enlarge 150 percent

LOVE POP-UP CARD

STYLISH
LANTERN

LOVE POP-UP CARD

SUPPLIES

1 sheet 120 g letter/A4 dark red paper · 1 sheet 120 g letter/A4 off-white paper
1 sheet half letter/A5 patterned paper · 1 piece tracing paper

MATERIALS

Scalpel · Cutter · Metal ruler · Paper-folding tool · Pencil
Embossing stylus · Cutting mat · Repositionable spray adhesive · Glue gel

DIRECTIONS

1) Photocopy the card pattern on a sheet of copy paper. Cut it out roughly, leaving a margin of about ¼ in. (5 mm).

2) Spray the back with repositionable spray adhesive. Apply it to the back of the sheet of red paper. The cut-out letters are inverted (see page 9). Smooth with your hand.

3) Cut the two vertical lines. Mark the folds: position the edge of the ruler along each dotted line. Mark the fold using the embossing stylus. Slide the paper-folding tool under the paper, pressing against the ruler to lift the paper and mark the fold. Remove the ruler. Use the paper-folding tool to flatten the crease. (See explanations on page 12.)

4) Cut out the letters using the cutter and ruler on the cutting mat. Remove the pattern.

5) Cut out a 2½ x 2½ in. (6.5 x 6.5 cm) square from the sheet of patterned paper. Glue it under the "L O V E" letters.

6) Trace and transfer the heart pattern to the back of the same paper, glued underneath the letters. Center and glue it to the bottom portion of the card.

7) Cut out a 3 15/16 x 7 5/8 in. (10 x 19.5 cm) rectangle from the sheet of off-white paper. Fold it in half and flatten the crease.

8) Apply glue gel to the outer edges of the card, without putting glue under the section with the letters. Apply it to the off-white card, making sure to center it and line it up with the middle creases. Let dry.

HEART
actual size

LOVE CARD
actual size

STYLISH LANTERN

SUPPLIES

1 sheet 120 g letter/A4 off-white paper
1 sheet 80 g letter/A4 patterned paper
1 sheet letter/A4 white corrugated cardboard
7⅞ in. (20 cm) fuchsia pink string

MATERIALS

Scalpel · Cutter · Metal ruler
Paper-folding tool · Pencil · Cutting mat
Repositionable spray adhesive
Glue gel

DIRECTIONS

1) Photocopy the lantern pattern on a sheet of copy paper.

2) Apply repositionable spray adhesive to the back. Glue it to the back of the sheet of off-white paper.

3) Cut out the red rectangles using the scalpel and metal ruler on the cutting mat.

4) Cut the vertical lines of the lantern using the metal ruler and cutter on the cutting mat. Cut out the contour. Mark the folds without flattening them.

5) Cut out two ½ x 7⅞ in. (1.5 x 20 cm) strips from the white corrugated cardboard. Glue each strip into a ring using glue gel.

6) Cut out a 3¹⁵⁄₁₆ x 7⅞ in. (10 x 20 cm) rectangle from the patterned paper.

7) Glue the top edge of the paper to the first ring of corrugated cardboard. Glue the second ring to the bottom edge of the paper to form a cylinder. Hang it until the glue has dried.

8) Glue the top edge of the off-white paper to the first ring of the cylinder, making sure to line up the edges. Hold it in place until the glue has dried. Repeat the procedure at the bottom of the cylinder; this will give the lantern more dimension. Hold it in place until the glue has dried.

9) Fold the fuchsia pink string in half. Glue both ends to the inside of the top ring, using two pieces of paper coated in glue gel. Hold them in place until the glue has dried.

LANTERN
actual size

TWO-COLORED BOXES

TWO-COLORED BOXES

SUPPLIES

1 sheet 120 g letter/A4 off-white paper
1 sheet 120 g letter/A4 golden yellow paper
1 sheet 120 g letter/A4 pink paper

MATERIALS

Scalpel · Cutter · Metal ruler · Paper-folding tool · Pencil
Cutting mat · Glue gel

DIRECTIONS

1) Print the pattern for the top part of the box on the off-white paper. Print the pattern for the bottom part of the box on the golden yellow paper.

2) Cut out the contour of the top part using the cutter and metal ruler on the cutting mat.

3) Mark the folds of the box: position the edge of the ruler along the dotted lines. Slide the paper-folding tool under the paper, pressing against the ruler to lift the paper and mark the fold. Remove the ruler. Use the paper-folding tool to flatten the creases. (See explanations on page 12 if needed.)

4) Place both elements on the cutting mat. Using the scalpel, cut out the inside pattern in yellow. Remove the cutout pieces gently.

5) Assemble the top part of the box. Apply glue gel to the flaps. Glue together and hold in place until the glue has dried.

6) Cut out the contour of the golden yellow part of the box using the cutter and metal ruler on the cutting mat.

7) Mark the folds.

8) Assemble the box and glue it together.

9) Place the top part of the box on the bottom part.

TOP
actual size

BOTTOM
actual size

The pink-and-
off-white box is
made according
to the same
procedure.

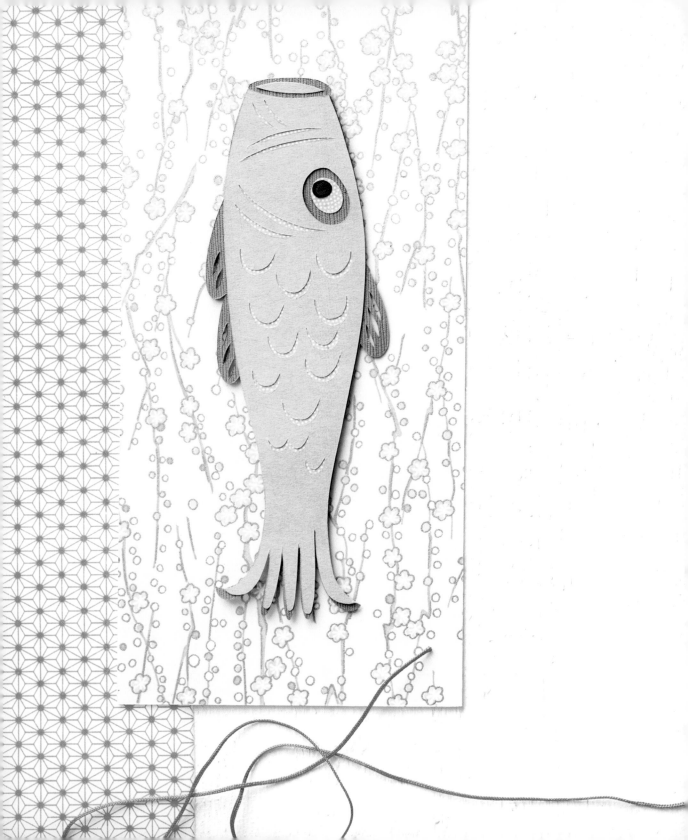

DEVELOPING SKILLS

Chapter 2

FLORAL
GIFT
DECORATION

Model no. 9

TERRARIUM

FLORAL GIFT DECORATION

SUPPLIES

1 sheet 160 g letter/A4 dark pink paper · 1 sheet 160 g letter/A4 raspberry pink paper
1 sheet letter/A4 tracing paper · 10 pale yellow paper flower pistils

MATERIALS

Scalpel · Cutter · Scissors · Paper-folding tool
Eyelet punch · Pencil · Cutting mat · Glue gel

DIRECTIONS

1) Photocopy the Flower no. 1 pattern on the sheet of pink paper.

2) Place the flower on the cutting mat. Using the scalpel, cut out the inner parts. Remove the pieces gently. Using the cutter, cut out the contour of the flower.

3) Enlarge, then trace the Flower no. 2 pattern. Cut out the contour using the cutter.

4) Fold the sheet of raspberry pink paper into eight. Draw a rounded tip as shown in the diagram below. Cut out the tip using scissors. Open the flower.

5) Pierce the center of both flowers using the eyelet punch.

6) Slide the pistils into the hole. Glue the stems to the back of the raspberry pink flower.

7) Glue the flowers in the following order: the flower in tracing paper, then the pink flower, and finally the small raspberry pink flower with the pistils. Glue the assembled flower to a gift box wrapped in decorative paper.

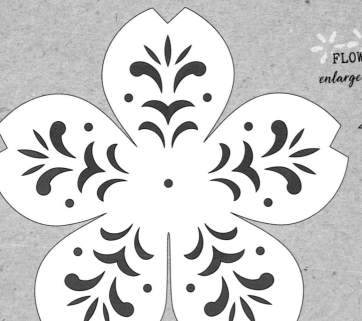

FLOWER NO. 2
enlarge 150 percent

FLOWER NO. I
enlarge 150 percent

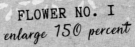

Tip: Trim the box with a strip of paper the same color as the flower in the center.

TERRARIUM

SUPPLIES

1 sheet 160 g half letter/A5 turquoise blue patterned paper · 1 sheet 160 g half letter/A5 anise green paper
1 sheet 160 g half letter/A5 almond green paper · 1 sheet 160 g half letter/A5 verdigris paper
1 sheet 160 g half letter/A5 celadon green paper · 1 sheet 160 g half letter/A5 eggplant paper
1 sheet 160 g half letter/A5 gray paper · 1 sheet 160 g 11.7 x 16.5 in/A3 khaki paper
1 sheet 200 g 11.7 x 16.5 in./A3 white paper · 1 sheet 120 g white paper

MATERIALS

Scalpel · Cutter · Metal ruler · Pencil
Cutting mat · Repositionable spray adhesive · Glue gel

DIRECTIONS

1) Photocopy the plant patterns on a sheet of 120 g white paper. Cut out the contour of the plants roughly, leaving a margin of about ⅜ in. (1 cm). Apply repositionable spray adhesive to the back. Glue each plant to a sheet of paper according to the color indicated on its pattern.

2) Place the turquoise blue plant on the cutting mat. Using the scalpel, cut out the inner parts. Remove the pieces gently. Cut out the inner parts of the eggplant-colored plant.

3) Glue the turquoise blue plant to the anise green paper. Cut out the contours again, using the cutter on the cutting mat. Set aside. Glue the eggplant-colored plant to the gray paper, then cut out the contours again.

4) Cut out the contours of the remaining plants, using the cutter on the cutting mat.

5) Measure a ³⁄₁₆ x 13 ¾ in. (3 x 35 cm) strip on the sheet of 200 g white paper. Glue on a strip of khaki paper of the same dimensions. Trace the slots, as indicated on page 49. Cut them out using the cutter and metal ruler on the cutting mat.

6) Glue the ends of the strip to form an oval ring.

7) Cut out a ³⁄₁₆ x 3 ¹⁵⁄₁₆ in. (0.5 x 10 cm) strip of anise green paper. Glue it to the khaki strip, between two slots.

8) Trace four strips on the sheet of 200 g white paper, according to the models on page 49. Cover one side with khaki paper. Trace the slots. Cut out the slots using the cutter and metal ruler on the cutting mat.

9) Glue each plant to its strip. Assemble the strips according to the corresponding slots.

TERRARIUM
enlarge 200 percent

荷
hé

lotus

はす

FISH KAKEMONO

SUPPLIES

1 sheet letter/A4 beige and blue patterned Japanese paper
1 sheet letter/A4 green and white patterned Japanese paper
1 sheet 80 g letter/A4 white paper · 1 sheet 200 g letter/A4 white paper
1 sheet half letter/A5 glazed chestnut paper · 1 sheet letter/A4 celadon green paper
1 sheet half letter/A5 dark red paper · 1 piece tracing paper
1 bamboo stick (16.3 cm long x 0.6 cm diameter)
1 fuchsia pink string (20 cm length)

MATERIALS

Scalpel · Cutter · Metal ruler · Pencil
Dark brown felt marker · Cutting mat · Repositionable spray adhesive
Permanent spray adhesive · Glue gel

DIRECTIONS

1) Photocopy all the fish patterns from page 53 on a sheet of 80 g white paper. Cut out each pattern roughly. Apply repositionable spray adhesive to the back of Fish no. 1. Glue it to the back of the celadon green paper. Smooth with your hand.

2) Place the fish on the cutting mat. Using the scalpel, cut out the inner parts. Remove the pieces gently. Cut out the contour of the fish and its mouth using the cutter. Remove the pattern.

3) Apply permanent spray adhesive to the back of the fish. Glue the fish to the sheet of green and white patterned Japanese paper. Smooth with your hand. Cut out the contour using the cutter on the cutting mat.

4) Apply repositionable spray adhesive to the back of Fish no. 2. Glue it to the back of the sheet of glazed chestnut paper. Smooth with your hand. Using the scalpel, cut out the fin patterns. Remove the pieces gently. Cut out the contour using the cutter. Remove the pattern.

5) Cut out the pattern of the strip of paper with flowers. Attach it to the glazed chestnut paper using masking tape. Cut out the flowers using the scalpel on the cutting mat. Glue a strip of green and white patterned Japanese paper under the cutout flowers.

MORE DIRECTIONS AND DIAGRAMS
on the next page

FISH KAKEMONO

CONTINUED FROM PREVIOUS PAGE

6) Cut out a 4⁵⁄₁₆ x 10⁷⁄₁₆ in. (11 x 26.5 cm) rectangle from the 200 g white paper. Apply permanent spray adhesive, then glue it to the sheet of beige and blue patterned Japanese paper. Smooth with your hand. Cut off the excess paper using the cutter and metal ruler on the cutting mat.

7) Place the rectangle vertically. Glue it to the top part of the strip of glazed chestnut paper. Add a strip of dark red paper measuring 1⅛ x 4⁵⁄₁₆ in. (3 x 11 cm) where the other two sheets of paper meet.

8) Glue the celadon green fish to the glazed chestnut fish. Glue the fish to the kakemono base. Trace the eye and pupil of the fish. Transfer the drawing of the eye to the back of the sheet of green and white patterned Japanese paper. Draw the pupil using the dark brown felt marker. Glue it onto the fish.

9) Cut two pieces of fuchsia pink string measuring 1½ in. (4 cm) in length. Fold the strings in half. Glue them to the back of the kakemono, ⅜ in. (1 cm) from the outside edge. Slide the bamboo stick through the strings. Fold the remaining piece of string in half and attach it to the middle of the bamboo stick to suspend the kakemono.

BROWN STRIP
actual size

POP-UP TREE

MY TIGER

POP-UP TREE

SUPPLIES

1 sheet 120 g 11.7 x 16.5 in./A3 lichen green paper
1 sheet 120 g letter/A4 almond green paper
1 sheet 80 g letter/A4 anise green patterned paper

MATERIALS

Scalpel · Cutter · Metal ruler
Paper-folding tool · Cutting mat · Permanent spray adhesive
Glue gel

DIRECTIONS

1) Photocopy the tree pattern twice on the sheet of almond green paper.

2) Mark the fold of the tree: position the edge of the ruler along the dotted line. Slide the paper-folding tool under the paper, pressing against the ruler to lift the paper and mark the fold. Remove the ruler. Use the paper-folding tool to flatten the crease.

3) Make the first tree. Apply permanent spray adhesive to the sheet of anise green patterned paper. Glue it to the back of the tree pattern, lined up at the fold. Smooth with your hand.

4) Place the tree on the cutting mat. Using the scalpel, cut out the inner parts. Remove the pieces gently. Cut out the contour using the cutter. Remove the pattern.

5) Make the back of the tree using the second photocopied tree. Mark the fold and cut out the inner parts using the scalpel.

6) Cut out a 5¾ x 12 in. (14.6 x 30.5 cm) rectangle from the sheet of lichen green paper. Fold it in half.

7) Using the glue gel, glue the two trees back to back, lining them up at the fold in the trunk. Glue both bases to the lichen green paper.

TREE (X2)
enlarge 145 percent

MY TIGER

SUPPLIES

1 sheet 120 g letter/A4 golden yellow paper
1 sheet 120 g letter/A4 brown paper
1 sheet 120 g letter/A4 pale yellow paper · 1 sheet 80 g letter/A4 gray and pink patterned paper
1 piece pink paper · 1 piece white paper

MATERIALS

Scalpel · Cutter · Metal ruler · Paper-folding tool · Pencil
Cutting mat · Permanent spray adhesive · Glue gel

DIRECTIONS

1) Photocopy the tiger elements on the sheet of golden yellow paper.

2) Mark the folds of the tiger's body: position the edge of the ruler along the dotted line. Slide the paper-folding tool under the paper, pressing against the ruler to lift the paper and mark the fold. Remove the ruler. Use the paper-folding tool to flatten the crease.

3) Place the tiger's body, head, and tail on the cutting mat. Using the scalpel, cut out the inner parts. Use the cutter to cut the slot for the tiger's tail. Remove the pieces gently. Cut out the contour using the cutter.

4) Apply permanent spray adhesive to the back of the tiger's body. Glue it to the sheet of brown paper, lined up with the folds on the feet. Smooth with your hand. Cut out the contour using the cutter on the cutting mat.

5) Draw six teeth on a piece of white paper, using the photo as a guide. Draw the nose on a piece of pink paper. Cut out the teeth and nose. Glue the teeth to the back of the tiger's head so they extend past the jaws. Glue on the pink nose.

6) Glue the tiger's head and tail to the sheet of brown paper. Smooth with your hand. Cut out the contour using the cutter on the cutting mat.

7) Transfer the measurements of the tab for the tiger's head to a piece of golden yellow paper. Cut out and mark the folds. Fold the tab according to the diagram, then glue it to the back of the tiger's head and body.

8) Slide the tiger's tail into the slot. Fold the base of the tail and use a drop of glue to attach it in back.

9) Cut out a 5¾ x 12 in. (14.6 x 30.5 cm) rectangle from the sheet of pale yellow paper. Using permanent spray adhesive, glue it to the sheet of gray and pink patterned paper. Apply glue gel to the feet and position them according to the place indicated on the card. Hold in place until the glue has dried.

TIGER HEAD, TAIL, AND BODY
enlarge 200 percent

CARD
(with positions for feet to be glued)
enlarge 200 percent

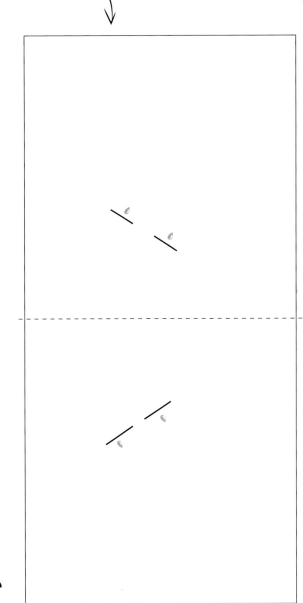

TEETH (X6)
& NOSE
actual size

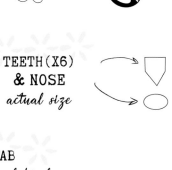

TAB
*(to glue behind
tiger's head)*
actual size

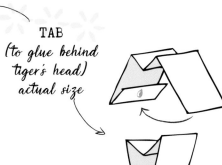

BIRD GARLAND

BIRD GARLAND

SUPPLIES

1 sheet half letter/A5 pink and white patterned Japanese paper
1 sheet half letter/A5 pink and white flower-patterned Japanese paper · 1 sheet letter/A4 raspberry pink paper
1 sheet half letter/A5 cream paper · 1 sheet half letter/A5 beige and white patterned paper
1 sheet 11.7 x 16.5 in./A3 almond green paper · 1 sheet tracing paper

MATERIALS

Scalpel · Cutter · Metal ruler · Paper-folding tool · Pencil
Cutting mat · Repositionable spray adhesive · Glue gel
Masking tape · Double-sided adhesive foam tape (¼ x ¼ in. [0.6 x 0.6 cm]) · Hole punch

DIRECTIONS

Flowers

1) Photocopy the A flower twice on a sheet of 80 g white paper. Cut them out roughly, leaving a margin of about ⅜ in. (1 cm). Apply repositionable spray adhesive to the back.

2) Apply the A1 flower to the back of the pink and white flower-patterned Japanese paper. Smooth with your hand. Apply the A2 flower to the back of the sheet of raspberry pink paper.

3) Cut out the contour of the raspberry pink flower. Glue it to the center of the pink Japanese paper flower.

4) Place it on the cutting mat. Using the scalpel, cut out the inner parts. Remove the pieces gently.

5) Remove the pattern. Glue the flower to the sheet of almond green paper. Cut off the excess paper. Set aside.

6) Prepare the rest of the flowers, one at a time, following the same procedure.

Leaves

1) Photocopy the patterns of the group of leaves and single leaves from page 63 on a sheet of almond green paper.

2) Place the leaf patterns on the cutting mat. Using the scalpel, cut out the inner parts. Cut out the contours using the cutter. Set aside.

MORE DIRECTIONS AND DIAGRAMS
on the next page

BIRD GARLAND

CONTINUED FROM PREVIOUS PAGE

Bird

1) Photocopy the frame for the bird. Position the pattern on the sheet of cream paper and hold it in place with masking tape. Place both elements on the cutting mat. Using the scalpel, cut out the parts shaded in gray, then gently remove them.

2) Cut out the inner and outer contour of the frame using the cutter.

3) Glue the frame to the sheet of pink and white patterned Japanese paper using glue gel. Cut off the excess paper using the cutter.

4) Photocopy the bird pattern. Position the pattern on the sheet of raspberry pink paper and hold it in place using masking tape. Place both elements on the cutting mat. Using the scalpel, cut out the eye and the wing.

5) Mark the fold of the wing. Cut out the silhouette of the bird using the cutter or scissors. Remove the pattern.

6) On the back of the bird, apply two squares of double-sided adhesive foam tape and attach the bird to the center of the frame.

Garland

1) Cut out a ⅜ x 16½ in. (1 x 42 cm) strip from the almond green paper. Trace the paper ring found on the opposite page. Transfer it to the almond green paper and cut it out.

2) Glue the ring to the end of the strip. Cut out an inverted "V" shape from the bottom of the strip.

3) Using the model in the photo as a guide, position the elements for the garland on the almond green strip before gluing them.

4) Glue the leaves to the strip and under the frame as shown. Add confetti from an office hole punch to the center of the second flower from the top.

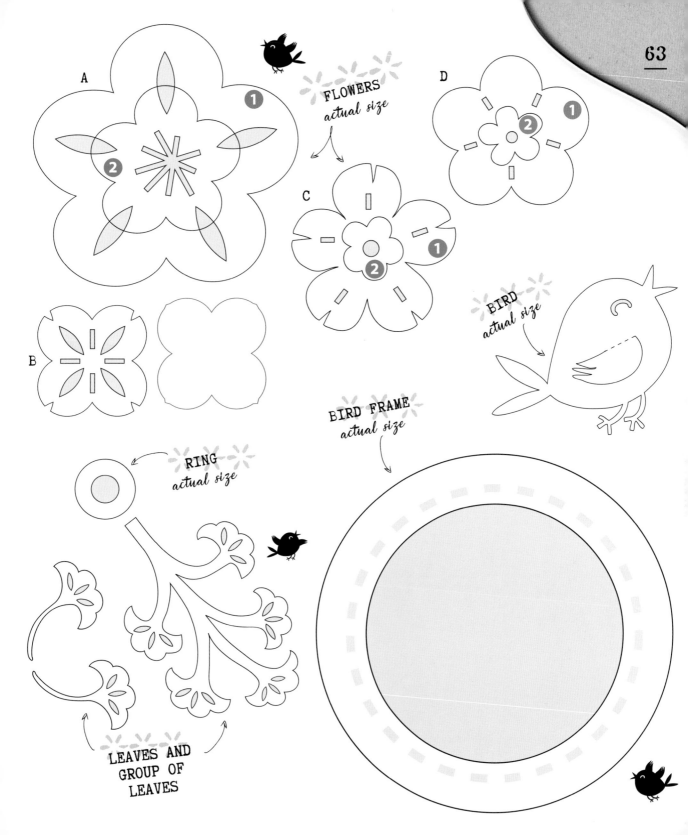

A

1

2

FLOWERS
actual size

D

1

2

C

1

2

B

BIRD
actual size

BIRD FRAME
actual size

RING
actual size

LEAVES AND
GROUP OF
LEAVES

BASKET

HERBARIUM

BASKET

SUPPLIES

1 sheet 160 g letter/A4 mauve paper
1 sheet 120 g half letter/A5 pale yellow paper

MATERIALS

Scalpel · Cutter · Metal ruler
Paper-folding tool · Pencil · Cutting mat
Glue gel

DIRECTIONS

1) Photocopy the basket pattern on the sheet of mauve paper. Make five photocopies of the star and diamond designs on the sheet of pale yellow paper.

2) Cut out the contour of the basket using the cutter and a metal ruler on the cutting mat.

3) Mark the folds for the basket: position the edge of the ruler along each dotted line. Slide the paper-folding tool under the paper, pressing against the ruler to lift the paper and mark the fold. Remove the ruler. Use the paper-folding tool to flatten the crease.

4) Place the pattern on the cutting mat. Using the scalpel, cut out the inner parts shaded in gray. Remove the pieces gently.

5) Cut out the inner parts of the stars using the cutter and metal ruler on the cutting mat. Cut out the contours, then the diamonds.

6) Glue the stars to the basket as shown in the photo. Add the diamonds.

7) Apply glue gel to the flaps. Assemble the basket and hold it in place until the glue has dried.

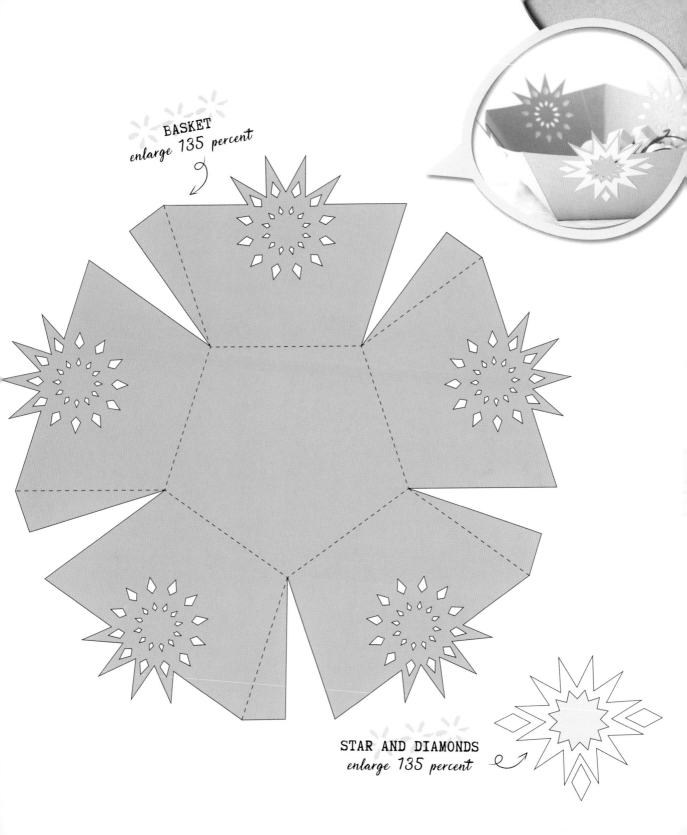

BASKET
enlarge 135 percent

STAR AND DIAMONDS
enlarge 135 percent

DEVELOPING SKILLS
DEVELOPING SKILLS

☙ HERBARIUM

SUPPLIES

1 sheet letter/A4 natural-color Kraft paper
1 sheet half letter/A5 celadon green paper · 1 sheet letter/A4 sky-blue patterned paper
1 sheet letter/A4 glazed chestnut paper · 1 piece tracing paper

MATERIALS

Scalpel · Cutter · Scissors · Metal ruler · Pencil
Glue · Cutting mat · Permanent spray adhesive · 1 fine-tip black felt marker

DIRECTIONS

1) Photocopy the plant patterns on the sheet of Kraft paper.

2) Place the plants on the cutting mat. Using the scalpel, cut out the inner parts. Remove the pieces gently. Cut out the contours using the scalpel.

3) Trace the silhouettes of the labels and transfer them to the back of the sheet of celadon green paper. Cut out using scissors. Write the names of the plants by hand on the labels using the fine-tip black felt marker. Set aside.

4) Cut out two 5 x 8 in. (12.6 x 20.5 cm) rectangles from the glazed chestnut paper. Cut out two 4 5/16 x 7 1/2 in. (11 x 19 cm) rectangles from the sky-blue patterned paper. Apply permanent spray adhesive to the sky-blue paper rectangles. Glue them to the center of the glazed chestnut paper rectangles.

5) Apply permanent spray adhesive to the plants. Center and glue them on each card. Add the labels to the stems of the corresponding plants.

PLANTS
actual size

1

2

LABELS
actual size

LITTLE CHALLENGES

JAPANESE CRANE

PINEAPPLE

Model no. 18

JAPANESE CRANE

SUPPLIES

1 sheet 120 g 5⅛ x 5⅛ in. (13 x 13 cm) ivory laid paper
1 sheet 120 g 5¾ x 5¾ in. (14.5 x 14.5 cm) cream handmade fiber-based paper
1 sheet 180 g 5¾ x 5¾ in. (14.5 x 14.5 cm) white paper

MATERIALS

Scalpel · Cutting mat
Repositionable spray adhesive · Permanent spray adhesive
Glue gel · Glue pen

DIRECTIONS

1) Photocopy the card pattern on a sheet of copy paper.

2) Apply repositionable spray adhesive to the back of the card. Apply the card to the back of the ivory laid paper. Smooth with your hand.

3) Cut out the flowers and petals using the scalpel on the cutting mat. Gently remove the cutout pieces.

4) Cut out the contour of the crane using the scalpel on the cutting mat. Gently remove the crane. Set aside. Remove the pattern.

5) Apply permanent spray adhesive to the sheet of cream paper. Center and apply it to the sheet of white paper. Smooth with your hand.

6) Glue the cutout ivory card onto the cream card using glue gel. Smooth with your hand.

7) Apply a thin line of glue to the body of the crane using the glue pen. Apply it to the position of the cutout crane. Hold in place by the wings until the glue has dried. Gently fold up the wings to make it three-dimensional.

JAPANESE CRANE
actual size

PINEAPPLE

SUPPLIES

1 sheet 120 g 5½ x 6⅞ in. (14 x 17.5 cm) dark gray paper
1 sheet 120 g 5⅛ x 6¾ in. (13 x 17 cm) copy paper
1 sheet 180 g letter/A4 5¾ x 7 in. (14.6 x 18 cm) white paper

MATERIALS

Scalpel · Cutter · Metal ruler
Pencil · Cutting mat · Paper-folding tool
Repositionable spray adhesive · Glue gel

DIRECTIONS

1) Photocopy the pineapple pattern on a sheet of copy paper.

2) Apply repositionable spray adhesive to the back. Glue it to the back of the sheet of dark gray paper. Smooth with your hand.

3) Cut out the parts shaded in gray using the scalpel on the cutting mat. Gently remove the cutout pieces.

4) Cut out the contour of the pineapple up to the fold line, using the scalpel on the cutting mat.

5) Mark the fold at the base of the pineapple. Position the edge of the ruler along the dotted line. Slide the paper-folding tool under the paper, pressing against the ruler to lift the paper and mark the fold. Remove the ruler. Use the paper-folding tool to flatten the crease. Gently remove the pattern.

6) On the back of the card, apply glue gel to the outer edge of the pineapple, without gluing the pineapple itself. Apply it to the printed paper, underneath the silhouette of the pineapple.

7) Apply permanent spray adhesive to the back of the card. Center and apply the card to the sheet of white paper. Smooth with your hand.

PINEAPPLE
actual size

GREETING CARD

Joyeux Noel

LANTERN

GREETING CARD

SUPPLIES

1 sheet 160 g letter/A4 white paper
1 sheet 200 g letter/A4 verdigris paper
1 piece green and gold patterned origami paper
1 piece 120 g dark red paper

MATERIALS

Scalpel · Cutter · Metal ruler · Pencil
Cutting mat · Repositionable spray adhesive
Glue gel or double-sided adhesive roller · Glue pen

DIRECTIONS

1) Photocopy the "Joyeux Noël" pattern on a sheet of 160 g white paper.

2) Start by cutting out the small loops in the letters using the scalpel on the cutting mat. Gently remove the cutout pieces.

3) Cut out the remaining inner parts of the letters using the scalpel on the cutting mat. Gently remove the cutout pieces.

4) Cut out the outer contour of all the letters using the scalpel on the cutting mat. Set aside.

LEAVES AND STAR

1) Photocopy the leaf and star patterns on a sheet of copy paper. Cut them out roughly, leaving a slight margin.

2) Apply repositionable spray adhesive to the back of the leaf and star patterns. Apply the leaves to the back of the piece of green and gold patterned origami paper. Apply the star to the back of the piece of red paper.

3) Cut out the inner parts of the star using the scalpel on the cutting mat. Gently remove the cutout pieces.

4) Cut out the outer contour of the star and leaves using the cutter on the cutting mat.

Assembly

1) Cut out a 6 ¹¹⁄₁₆ x 9⁷⁄₁₆ in. (17 x 24 cm) rectangle from the sheet of verdigris paper. Position the leaves, lettering, and star in an attractive arrangement, using the model in the photo as a guide.

2) Coat the back of the "Joyeux Noël" with glue using the glue pen. Apply it to the sheet of verdigris paper. Smooth with your hand. Add the two leaves and the star last.

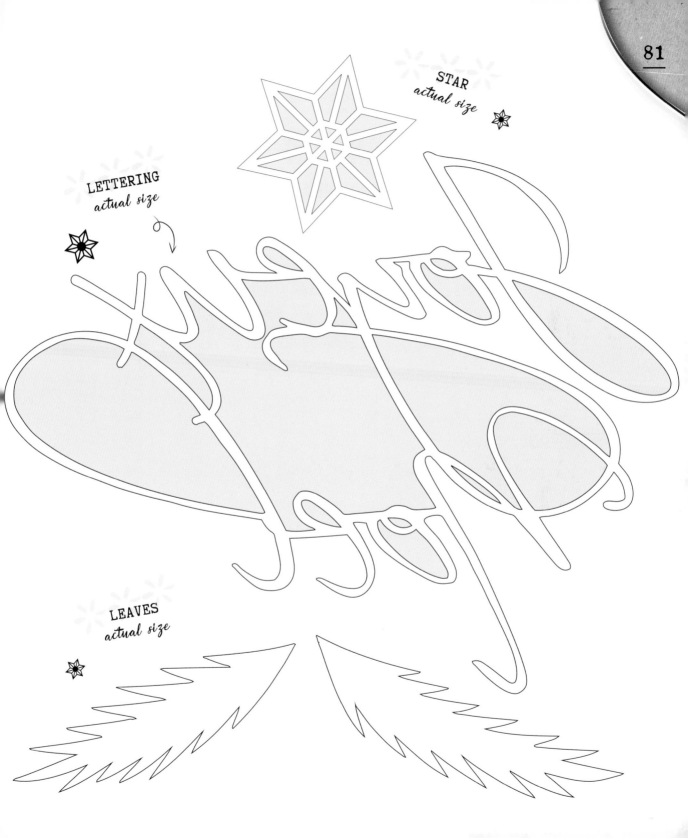

STAR
actual size

LETTERING
actual size

LEAVES
actual size

LANTERN

SUPPLIES

1 sheet 80 g letter/A4 ivory laid paper
1 sheet letter/A4 white corrugated cardboard
1 sheet letter/A4 tracing paper

MATERIALS

Scalpel · Cutter · Metal ruler · Pencil
Cutting mat · Repositionable spray adhesive · Permanent spray adhesive
Glue gel or double-sided adhesive roller

DIRECTIONS

1) Photocopy the lantern pattern on a sheet of copy paper.

2) Apply repositionable spray adhesive to the back. Glue it to the back of the sheet of ivory laid paper. Smooth with your hand.

3) Cut out the designs using the scalpel on the cutting mat. Gently remove the cutout pieces.

4) Cut out the contour of the lantern using the cutter and metal ruler on the cutting mat. Remove the pattern.

5) Apply permanent spray adhesive to the back of the lantern. Glue it to the sheet of tracing paper. Smooth with your hand. Cut off excess paper.

6) Cut out a ⁹⁄₁₆ x 7⅞ in. (1.5 x 20 cm) strip of white corrugated cardboard and form a ring. Apply glue gel to hold the ring.

7) Glue the bottom edge of the lantern, on the side of the tracing paper, to the ring of corrugated cardboard. Glue it at the top to close the cylinder. Let dry.

Place an LED candle
or a real candle in
a glass jar inside
the lantern.

LANTERN
enlarge 125 percent

Model no. 21

PAPER LACE
DOILIES

ASIAN
TEMPLE

PAPER LACE DOILIES

SUPPLIES

1 sheet 120 g half letter/A5 raspberry pink paper
1 sheet 120 g half letter/A5 dark red paper
1 sheet 120 g half letter/A5 verdigris paper
1 sheet 120 g half letter/A5 khaki paper

MATERIALS

Scalpel · Cutter · Eyelet punch
Cutting mat · Repositionable spray adhesive
Glue gel or double-sided adhesive roller

DIRECTIONS

1) Photocopy the patterns of the flowers and leaves on a sheet of copy paper. Cut out each piece roughly, leaving a slight margin.

2) Apply repositionable spray adhesive to each pattern. Apply one flower to the back of the sheet of raspberry pink paper and the other flower to the back of the sheet of red paper. Smooth with your hand. Apply the leaves to the back of the sheets of verdigris and khaki paper.

3) Cut out the designs from the flowers, starting with the petals in the center, using the scalpel on the cutting mat. Gently remove the cutout pieces.

4) Cut out the holes in the middle of Flower no. 1 using the eyelet punch.

5) Cut out the contour of the flowers using the scalpel on the cutting mat.

6) Cut out the veins of the leaves, starting in the center, using the scalpel. Gently remove the cutout pieces. Cut out the contours of the leaves.

7) Glue the leaves under the outer edges of the flowers using glue gel or double-sided adhesive roller.

FLOWER NO. 1
actual size

FLOWER NO. 2
actual size

X3

LEAVES
actual size

X2

ASIAN TEMPLE

SUPPLIES

1 sheet 80 g letter/A4 turquoise blue Kraft paper
1 sheet 120 g letter/A4 turquoise blue paper
1 sheet 120 g letter/A4 deep blue patterned paper
1 sheet 5 5⁄16 x 10 5⁄8 in. (13.5 x 27 cm) turquoise blue paper

MATERIALS

Scalpel · Cutter · Metal ruler · Pencil
Cutting mat · Repositionable spray adhesive · Embossing stylus
Paper-folding tool · Glue gel or double-sided adhesive roller
Permanent spray adhesive

DIRECTIONS

1) Photocopy the temple pattern on the sheet of turquoise blue paper.

2) Apply permanent spray adhesive to the back. Glue it to the back of the sheet of turquoise blue Kraft paper. Smooth with your hand.

3) Cut out the outer contour of the temple using the scalpel and ruler on the cutting mat.

4) Mark the folds: position the edge of the ruler along each dotted line. Mark the fold using the embossing stylus. Slide the paper-folding tool under the paper, pressing against the ruler to lift the paper and mark the fold. Remove the ruler. Use the paper-folding tool to flatten the crease. (See explanations on page 12.)

5) Cut out the inner parts of the temple using the cutter and ruler on the cutting mat. Cut out the stars.

6) Cut out a 4 ¾ x 5 15⁄16 in. (12 x 15 cm) rectangle from the sheet of deep blue patterned paper. On the back of the card, coat the contour of the temple with glue gel, making sure not to glue the temple itself. Apply it to the sheet of deep blue patterned paper.

7) Fold the 5 5⁄16 x 10 5⁄8 in. (13.5 x 27 cm) sheet of turquoise blue paper in half.

8) Apply glue gel to the outer edges of the card. Glue it to the sheet of blue paper, making sure to center it and line it up with the central fold. Let dry.

TEMPLE
enlarge 140 percent

The symbol

1) Photocopy the symbol pattern on a sheet of turquoise blue paper.

2) Apply permanent spray adhesive to the back of the pattern. Glue it to the back of the sheet of deep blue patterned paper. Smooth with your hand.

3) Cut out the inner parts using the cutter and ruler on the cutting mat. Cut out the outer contour.

4) Center and glue the symbol on the lower section of the card.

3D CARD

PARISIAN BRIDGE

3D CARD

SUPPLIES

1 sheet 160 g 11.7 x 16.5 in./A3 cream paper
1 sheet 120 g letter/A4 yellow polka-dot paper
1 sheet 120 g letter/A4 turquoise blue paper

MATERIALS

Scalpel · Cutter · Metal ruler · Pencil
Cutting mat · Repositionable spray adhesive · Paper-folding tool
Permanent spray adhesive · Glue gel or double-sided adhesive roller

DIRECTIONS

1) Trace a 5⁵⁄₁₆ x 16 in. (13.5 x 40.5 cm) rectangle in the sheet of cream paper. Cut out using the cutter and metal ruler on the cutting mat. Fold the sheet into three.

2) Photocopy the two patterns on a sheet of copy paper. Cut out the contour of the squares using the cutter and metal ruler.

3) Apply repositionable spray adhesive to the back. Glue Element no. 1 to the interior left side of the cream card. Apply Element no. 2 to the interior right side. Smooth with your hand.

4) Cut out the arcs of the circles to be lifted using the scalpel on the cutting mat.

5) Mark the folds of the arcs of the circles: position the edge of the ruler along the dotted lines. Slide the paper-folding tool under the arc of the circles, pressing against the ruler to lift the paper. Remove the ruler. Use the paper-folding tool to flatten the creases.

6) Cut out the parts shaded in gray using the scalpel on the cutting mat. Gently remove the cutout pieces. Remove the pattern.

7) Apply permanent spray adhesive to the back of the sheet of yellow polka-dot paper. Center and glue it to the right side of the card, which is the side opposite to the pattern. Smooth with your hand. Cut off excess paper.

8) Cut out the crosses shaded in gray using the scalpel on the cutting mat. Gently remove the cutout pieces. Remove the pattern.

9) Cut out a 5⅛ x 5⅛ in. (13 x 13 cm) square from the sheet of turquoise blue paper and glue it under the cutout crosses using glue gel. Let dry.

10) Fold the card in three and gently open the arcs of the circles to make the card three-dimensional.

ELEMENT NO. 2
enlarge 140 percent

PARISIAN BRIDGE

SUPPLIES

1 sheet 160 g letter/A4 blue-gray paper
1 sheet 160 g letter/A4 deep blue paper
1 sheet 160 g letter/A4 turquoise blue paper
1 sheet letter/A4 deep blue and gold dotted origami paper
1 sheet 200 g letter/A4 white paper · 1 piece gold glitter paper

MATERIALS

Scalpel · Cutter · Metal ruler · Pencil
Cutting mat · Repositionable spray adhesive
Glue gel or double-sided adhesive roller · Embossing stylus
Paper-folding tool · Disc cutter with ⅝ in. (1.6 cm) diameter punch

DIRECTIONS

Paris skyline

1) Photocopy the pattern of the Paris skyline on a sheet of copy paper.

2) Apply repositionable spray adhesive to the back. Glue it to the back of the sheet of blue-gray paper. Smooth with your hand.

3) Mark the folds: position the edge of the ruler along each dotted line. Mark the fold using the embossing stylus. Slide the paper-folding tool under the paper, pressing against the ruler to lift the paper and mark the fold. Use the folding tool to flatten the crease.

4) Cut out the windows of the skyline using the scalpel on the cutting mat. Gently remove the cutout pieces.

5) Cut out the silhouette of the skyline using the scalpel on the cutting mat. Gently remove the cutout pieces.

6) Cut out the outer contour of the remaining elements using the cutter and metal ruler on the cutting mat. Remove the pattern.

7) Coat the back of the Paris skyline with glue gel. Apply it to the sheet of blue and gold dotted origami paper. Smooth with your hand. Cut out the contours that extend past the edges. Cut out the moon from gold glitter paper using the disc cutter. Glue the moon to the sky.

8) Reinforce the base by gluing it to the sheet of 200 g 6¼ x 7 in. (16 x 18 cm) white paper. Mark the fold ¾ in. (2 cm) from the bottom.

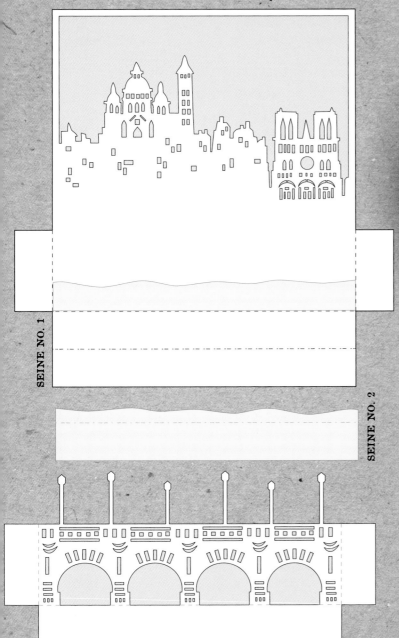

CARD BASE
enlarge 200 percent

SEINE NO. 1

SEINE NO. 2

BRIDGE
enlarge 200 percent

Bridge

1) Photocopy the bridge pattern on a sheet of copy paper. Cut it out roughly, leaving a slight margin.

2) Apply repositionable spray adhesive to the back. Glue it to the back of the sheet of deep blue paper. Smooth with your hand.

3) Mark the folds: position the edge of the ruler along each dotted line. Slide the paper-folding tool under the paper, pressing against the ruler to lift the paper and mark the fold. Remove the ruler. Use the paper-folding tool to flatten the crease.

4) Cut out the details of the bridge using the scalpel on the cutting mat. Gently remove the cutout pieces.

5) Cut out the silhouette of the bridge using the scalpel on the cutting mat. Remove the pattern.

The Seine (River)

1) Print the two patterns of the Seine on a sheet of turquoise blue paper.

2) Mark the folds: position the edge of the ruler along each dotted line. Slide the paper-folding tool under the paper, pressing against the ruler to lift the paper and mark the fold. Remove the ruler. Use the paper-folding tool to flatten the creases.

3) Cut out the two silhouettes of the Seine using the cutter on the cutting mat.

Assembly

1) Glue the Seine no. 1 element to the base of the skyline, lined up with the fold line, using the glue pen.

2) Glue the Seine no. 2 element behind the bridge, lined up with the fold lines.

3) Coat the flaps of the bridge with glue gel. Attach them to the flaps of the base, using the diagram as a guide. Let dry.

ACKNOWLEDGMENTS

Many thanks to dynamic duo Vania and Fabrice for these magnificent and inspiring photos . . .
and to Adeline, for your continued assurance and joy in making such beautiful books!

DESIGN ACKNOWLEDGMENTS

Adeline Klam *www.adelineklam.com*
Hema *www.hema.fr*
Dodo Toucan *www.dodo-toucan.com*
Muji *www.muji.com/fr*
Petit Pan *www.petitpan.com*
Toraya *www.toraya-group.co.jp/toraya-paris*

ADDRESSES

Origami paper

Adeline Klam: *www.adelineklam.com*

Paper and materials

L'éclat de verre: *www.eclatdeverre.com*
Rougier & Plé: *www.rougier-ple.fr*
Toga: *www.toga-shop.com*

Project Team (Fox Chapel Publishing Edition)

Vice President – Content: Christopher Reggio
Translator: Donna Vekteris
Editor: Jeremy Hauck
Layout: David Fisk

Project Team (French Edition)

Editorial Director: Thierry Lamarre
Editor: Adeline Lobut
Proofreader: Isabelle Misery
Project Design/Construction and Step-by-Step Directions: Ghylenn Descamps
Photography: Fabrice Besse
Stylist: Vania Leroy-Thuillier
Design and Layout: Either Studio/Damien Payet

Mes premiers pas en kirigami © 2017 by Editions Marie Claire – Société d'Information et Créations (SIC). English translation published 2019, under the title *Beginner's Guide to Kirigami*, by Fox Chapel Publishing, 903 Square Street, Mount Joy, PA 17552.

ISBN 978-1-4971-0016-9

The Cataloging-in-Publication data is on file with the Library of Congress.

To learn more about the other great books from Fox Chapel Publishing, or to find a retailer near you, call toll-free 800-457-9112 or visit us at *www.FoxChapelPublishing.com*.

We are always looking for talented authors. To submit an idea, please send a brief inquiry to acquisitions@foxchapelpublishing.com.

Printed in China
First printing